THE TUTOR

My Journey as an Adult Volunteer Literacy Tutor

DAVID JAMES BOYCE, JR.

The Reading Glass Books
1-888-420-3050
www.readingglassbooks.com
fulfillment@readingglassbooks.com

Table of Contents

MEET THE AUTHOR

DAVID JAMES BOYCE, JR. is a retired military veteran with over twenty-seven years of service. He enlisted in the U.S. Army in December 1968 before graduating high school. He was adamant about continuing his education because he felt that was one thing he could apply to his life and share with others. After graduating high school, from Saint Louis High School, Honolulu, HI while stationed on his first tour in Korea, Boyce continued his education earning his Associate of Science from Georgia Military College, Georgia, a Bachelor of Science degree in Human Resource Management from Empire State College in New York, and a master's degree in Education from Trident University, California. His tutoring certifications include Tutor, Master Tutor, Tutor Trainer, and Master Tutor Trainer-Literacy.

This work, entitled My Journey as an Adult Literacy Volunteer Tutor chronicles my path, and what I have learned to help adult non-readers become more independent after learning to read.

Teaching is the one thing that can only be paid forward, and the benefits last a lifetime. This reflects the lens of his passion, calling for volunteering and teaching adult non-readers to read, write, and improve their life skills. He has been tutoring new adult learners since 1986.

PREFACE

"Make a difference about something other than yourselves."
-Toni Morrison

The purpose of this book is to educate the reader on our unseen continuously growing **illiteracy** problem and some of the issues that affect non-reading adults today in our communities and possibly in some of our homes. I wrote this book to share my experiences with fellow tutors, community leaders to share my experiences of tutoring non-reading adults to help them read, write, and assist them in the improvement of their lives since 1986. This journey currently spans more than three decades of volunteer service to date in communities as an Adult Literacy Volunteer Tutor in and out of the military. "**Illiteracy** has been present in American lives since the foundation of this country, and unfortunately is still around today" (Impacts of **Illiteracy**, n. d.). Simply stated, **illiteracy** means not being able to read or write in one's dominant or command language, skill, or profession. The adult **illiteracy** rate in the United States is continuing to rise and the issue is becoming more pervasive year after year. "In 1980, the U.S. Census Bureau counted 24.3 million Americans over the age of 25 who had not gone beyond the 8th grade" (New Readers Press, 1989). That number has increased by 18.7 million persons to 43 million U. S. adults with low literacy skills (OECD 2013). If these numbers representing **illiteracy** were an illness or disease, they would be declared an epidemic, which requires time, effort, and resources to correct the situation. 8.2 million adults are classified as functionally illiterate, not able to understand short bits of information. Low literacy rates cost the affected individuals to our nation trillions of dollars in terms of economic impact.

I have tutored adults in Germany, Hagerstown and Frederick, Maryland; Calcium and Fort Drum, New York; Phoenix City, Alabama, Hinesville and Columbus, Georgia. Overseas assignments also provided tutoring opportunities in Frankfurt, Germany through the Army Community Services program.

I hope that readers of this book find space in their hearts and schedules to help change an adult's life by volunteering to tutor someone to read, write, and improve their life skills. Although the strategies in this book are used primarily with adults, one can also use these strategies, guides, and materials with younger learners as I did with my last three children while they were in grade school. The **information** and strategies that I have learned, researched, taught, and shared can be valuable assets for parents teaching their school-age children. Compare the school-age children at home unable to get a parent's assistance with homework because their parent has difficulties reading. In addition, providing insights and a springboard for adults learning to read and write beyond school age helps the entire family unit.

The objective of this book is to encourage volunteers to help adult non-readers become proficient at the fifth grade reading level and accomplish life skill tasks for their needs in their daily lives. This is the minimum requirement for those that want to continue and enroll in an Adult Basic Education (ABE) program to achieve a General Education Diploma (GED). Today, more than ever, adult literacy tutors are needed in every community. My mission is to help as many adults as possible who want to learn, change their lives and improve their family's life.

VOLUNTEER to **TUTOR** a non-reading adult and help
CHANGE their **LIFE** and **FUTURE.**

INTRODUCTION

"The time is always right to do the right thing."

-Martin Luther King, Jr.

What do you want to be when you grow up? As a child, I was often asked that question, by family members and other **adults**, even some teachers. The answer came when I saw someone that I liked, on a weekend television show or what I saw someone do in the community. My answers ranged from a police officer, firefighter, truck driver, teacher, and then an airplane driver, as I knew then. As I gave those answers to the **adults'** questions there seemed to be an image in my mind seeing myself in those positions. Arresting the bad people; putting out fires; driving big trucks; and driving an airplane through the clouds looking down at small buildings. It felt good. In school, other **possibilities** emerged, when our class went to the school library each week. I would ask and get help to find a book to read about some grownup professions.

As a child, we learned to read by hearing the word, looking at the picture, sounding out the word with assistance, and saying the word. Later, we learn to spell and write the words. Hearing, speaking, saying, and writing the word is a process we learn from childhood. As we proceed through this process, **comprehension** helps us build and use our vocabulary skills. Advancing from single words to sentences and later writing notes and letters. Some words may have the same beginning sound although they begin with different letters. For example, look at the words car and kite. Note: the c and k have the same beginning sound; however, the letters are different. Note: the letter c has the same beginning sound in the illustrated words; yet the c in the word like cent has a softer sound.

Reading was a way for me to travel the world, converse with people, and have conversations by turning pages of a good book and daydreaming about the experience. Imagine sitting on a mountaintop like Jesus or driving a fast car without fear or danger turning curves in tight bends, going full-throttle on a racetrack. I could be sitting on distant riverbanks fishing with a fancy rod and reel with the best lures around musing about those prized catches. This is possible through the pages of a book. Helping others spell and read better was a skill that I developed in grade school. In the classroom, assisting other students with spelling and sounding out words (phonics as I learned later) brought many "thanks" from many of my classmates. "As every man hath received the gift, even so, minister the same one to another, as good stewards of the manifold grace of God" (I Peter 4:10) King James Version. We all have a skill or talent that can enrich someone else's life by sharing. Be that beacon of light to help at least one person improve their lives and the lives of their family. Once planted, that seed grows to fruition, the harvest will spread beyond one's imagination. Pass it on. Our home, community, and nation benefit from our collective efforts to enrich the lives of others. The life we live is a journey. We are born to learn, journey, and leave. No one walks alone nor struggles on this journey alone, but in the end, we all meet the same fate.

Teaching adults to read, write, and improve their life skills have been my passion since October 1986. Adults with low literacy skills will continue to affect us for generations to come if we do nothing to help those that truly want to learn. Not only the **adult** but also the household, employer, community, and the nation benefit from the improvement. Imagine not being able to read to or help your child with their studies in Pre-K, elementary school, and beyond. Some non-reading adults may make excuses or send their children back to the teacher if there is no one available to assist in the family. An adult being able to help their child with academic work and social skills empowers the adult and child.

To date, I have tutored adults for more than thirty-five years. During that time, there has not been a lack of students wanting to learn. Ads placed on street corners, in magazines and newspapers, are fruitless to the non-reading adult. They simply look beyond these signs. If you know anyone needing literacy training, find an organization, and encourage him or her to improve his or her life by learning to read and write if that is what he or she desires.

Although my journey is tutoring and empowering non-reading adults. I have also worked part-time as a Substitute Teacher in our local school district for over three years. Some children experience some of the same challenges in the classroom and adults experience in life situations. No matter our passion for teaching-learning, we work and share our experiences as a team. The goal is to help as many students as possible and adults improve their level of competency to excel I their life's situations.

The **tutor** treats and respects each adult as an adult. The student must first be able to push their pride aside and ask for help. At this point, worlds of possibilities begin to emerge. Tutoring adults to learn to read and as they progress, they read to learn propelling them into life skills and move towards high school and beyond. Please note, wherever you see a word in bold type you can see that word in the glossary in the back of the book. The definitions are explained to help the reader understand the context in which it was used.

DEDICATION

"They came because they wished to learn."

-Frederick Douglass

Before moving forward, it is important to see how low-literate or non-literate adults use their system of survival skills. Some are employed, manage households and raise families. Others operate businesses and even volunteer in our communities where we live daily. As tutors, we learn from each other and our shared experiences. For adults desiring to improve their experiences enters a new phase of development learning new skills and elevating the competency of new tasks. Literacy tutors now more than ever are needed as technology continues to evolve requiring more proficiency skills and less direct supervision.

I wrote this book to honor individuals, families, educators, friends, tutor trainers, tutors, and emerging adult readers. Where I am today is a culmination of my life experiences and the people that have assisted me, and those I have learned from on this long journey and assisted along the way. To date, I have donated eight to 10,000 hours of free volunteer tutoring services to empower new adult learners, helping them improve themselves and move forward to achieve their desired goals. My purpose in writing this book is to help those reading below grade level. According to statista.com, the Jan 7, 2021, the National voter turnout rate was 66.7 percent as of December 7, 2020, for the presidential election. The voter turnout statistics was recorded as the highest ever. Imagine what the rate may have been had the additional 43 million English-speaking, eligible, non-reading adult population were reading, writing, registering, and voting their convictions.

CHAPTER

I

WHY LEARN TO READ?

"Not everything that is faced can be changed, but nothing can be changed until it is faced."

-James Baldwin

Literacy is the basis of all other types of education. Our education system is comprised of two primary education platforms. They are formal and non-formal education. Formal foundation education is conducted primarily through schools, colleges, and universities that provide grade-level instruction. Schools and colleges are accredited as Regional, National, Faith-based, Technical, Program, and Special accreditation. Academic subjects are delivered and taught by trained, degreed, certified professional educators, and technical instructors. Most hands-on skills, i.e., welding, building trades, truck driving professionals, medical careers, and others are classified as technical **training**. The compulsory age ranges for formal education is 5 to 18. Some states have compulsory maximum ages up to 16 years of age.

Non-formal education is on a different platform. Non-formal education is **learned** from one's home, social environment, life experiences, work, peers, and family units. Age ranges for non-formal education are from birth and progress throughout one's life. "Non-formal education is flexible; it adapts its content and methods to the wants and needs of its stakeholders (initiators, teachers, participants. (Moser, 1996:140)." Statistically, adults with weak literacy skills are more likely to live in poverty, "some work off the book", do not participate in our political process, become and remain unemployed, struggle to complete employment applications, misunderstand technology, and struggle to support their family. There are many reasons why people do not go back to school. They range from a necessity to work or a lack of interest maybe due to other challenges. Tutoring adults to read and write falls within the area of non-formal education.

This portion of non-formal education is provided by literacy organizations and other volunteer agencies in which are mostly operated and staffed mainly by **volunteers**. There is little if any direct funding from the Federal and some state governments. Major funding comes in the form of grants, **philanthropic** organizations, and individual **donors**. Once adults obtain 5th grade-level competency, some can enroll in General Education Development (GED) **programs** to complete their high school equivalency diploma (The History of the GED (n. d.). Some technical schools offer certificate programs for adults to enter the workforce through technical **training** that does not require a high school diploma. Many of these programs are for hands-on training, such as Forklift Operator and others. Even today in 2022, millions of adults do not know how to read and **write**. Often, when one must feed their family, education is not a priority for many adults. Survival and putting food on the table becomes the number one issue for the adult provider in the family.

Learning to **read** involves the process of letter identification, sound, phonics, building words, spelling, sentence structure, and punctuation. Reading is the platform that propels the reader to explore adventures in unknown places, **learn** new things, prepare for various situations, and advance life choices all from the pages of a good book. Reading to your children helps them learn to pronounce words, converse about pictures on the pages, and most of all that warm feeling of bonding with having uninterrupted alone time between parent and child. That is "priceless".

CHAPTER

II

MY CALLING

"Today, a reader, tomorrow a leader."
– Margaret Fuller

Many of us have one calling, recognized, or not. It sometimes takes you longer to find your calling than others. My calling was to answer the question. What will you give to help others? As a **nonreader**, how would you know which product to buy if there were no pictures? Consider looking at a plain **label** with no product picture and you cannot read? A plain black and white label identifying the product is like a sighted person blindfolded. Now imagine if you are an adult, cannot **read**, **write**, or understand the written word in the world around you. When you cannot read and write, others often make decisions for you. Some of those decisions may be good, bad, or not in your best interest. As a result, the non-reading **adult** suffers from decisions that are not completed for their benefit or decisions that they do not fully understand. All can **learn** and improve our world.

How would you be able to understand which **medicine** to take or worse, give the wrong medicine in the incorrect amount to yourself or someone in your **household**? These issues and others affect many nonreaders and their **households** daily. Some non-reading adults take menial, physically demanding jobs or work under the table (without any **deductions** or **benefits**) for cash only, rather than getting a W-2 Form or Form 1099 for tax purposes at the end of the year to file an income tax return. Because of these actions, no income tax filings for income, no contributions to their Social Security account for possible future disability or retirement benefits, no company benefits, no medical or dental **insurance** for their family, and no funding for a savings or retirement account. Once an illness strikes, nonreaders often go to an emergency room or urgent medical care facility for medical attention because they lack medical insurance or a primary care doctor to care for periodic and routine medical issues.

For example, some adult non-readers can adapt to their situational surroundings by memory, cognitive, visual clues, and enabled by other adults. Businesses have developed various ways to assist nonreaders by marketing to sell their products and services. A restaurant, for example, displays menu boards with pictures and corresponding numbers to select. We look at menu boards and select a number one or number four. In stores, merchandise packaging shows pictures of enclosed contents and see-through packaging film. Milk producers no longer use uniform markings for milk in stores. In grocery stores, color codes are in the dairy section. Color-coded caps, i.e. red, whole milk, and blue for two percent milk, etc., for example, identify the type of milk in the containers. Recently shopping for whole milk, I found a red cap and a yellow label. Two-percent milk had a blue cap and a green label. Some are marked with a blue cap and a blue label. If a non-reading consumer purchases the wrong milk product, once it leaves the store, that product cannot be returned or exchanged. Ads and marketing strategies lead many non-readers to buy the wrong product or spend more money on purchases due to a lack of knowledge of comparison-shopping.

Literacy, defined, as the ability to read and write in one's language. For the adult that cannot read, write, or have a command of **numeracy** skills in their language they struggle for themselves and their family. They are lost and must depend on someone they trust for assistance. Most low-level reading adults hide what they perceive as shame and constantly look for reasons why a task cannot be completed or express why they dislike the task. Without basic literacy skills, employment as a laborer is often out of reach. This also places nonreaders at risk of using medications incorrectly, or not being able to understand various bills or contracts that affect their household budget and livelihood.

My calling came in October 1986. On that afternoon, off work, I sat watching Oprah's daytime talk show. I remember Dennis Weaver was a guest. They were appealing for adults to volunteer, receive local literacy training, and become an Adult Volunteer Literacy Tutor to help non-reading adults learn to read and write and improve their situation. Mr. Weaver was also announcing his upcoming TV movie, "Bluffing It" (Sadwith, J. 1987). He "Duggan," played the part of a supervisor in an automotive plant and was given the task of reducing the workforce by laying off some of his subordinates due to automation upgrades. The new computer operations would make the remaining employee's jobs easier and more productive. Some workers were **retained**, in their current position. However, Duggan had a secret that would keep him from doing his new job and he was afraid that if anyone found out that he could not read, his life would be ruined. His family did not know. Rather than admit his secret, he resigned in protest of the layoffs". His secret: he was functionally illiterate. That means that he did not possess the literacy skills to function independently without an enabler. This factory supervisor now loses his job after refusing a promotion that required reading and computer literacy skills.

While watching this program, in the back of my mind, I heard, "You can do this, help us. Help us please!" I knew then that this was my calling. Excited, I called the 800 number, provided some **information**, and was referred to a local Literacy Council in my area. The qualifications were good reading and writing skills, completing the 12 to 14-hour workshop, and committing to tutoring one student for six months. The Frederick County Literacy Council was about 29 miles away from my residence at Fort Ritchie, MD. After learning the location, length of the course, and requirements I was set.

CHAPTER

III

TUTOR TRAINING

"Reading is a basic tool in the living of a good life."
– Mortimer J. Adler

During our two-day Tutor Training Workshop, we were trained and taught; how to conduct our tutoring sessions; more importantly, the psychological aspects of how a non-reader feels asking for help. To illustrate, we were blindfolded so we could understand how a person feels as they try to survive in their various social settings. Place yourself in a vulnerable position. How does it feel to be helpless? Next, we learned how to assess the student's reading and writing ability to prepare a starting point for tutoring and acquire materials that would be used and how to be sensitive to our student's needs.

The Laubach Way to Reading series used contains Skill Levels 1–4 materials. That includes the primary book and two storybooks called correlated readers written on the accompanying skill level. Each Skill Level also includes a Focus on Phonics series that aids in phonics, word skill development, learning word families, and patterns in spelling. Once the student completes all four levels, he or she would be reading on at least the 5th-grade level. The whole class was enthusiastic and ready to become literacy tutors and help adult nonreaders in our communities. This will help improve the new readers in all areas of their life to be more productive.

Training volunteers for this program was **established** using New Readers Press literacy materials (New Readers Press, 2012). This training covered four reading skill levels including levels 1, 2, 3, and 4 with student and teacher editions. Tutor training consists of volunteers completing a 12-hour tutor certification workshop (Tutor Training Guide, n.d.) that **focused** on teaching basic reading and writing, listening skills from zero levels up to fifth grade. Each of the four levels consists of a detailed teacher's manual, a student skill book, a correlated reader, checkups, and a diploma (Laubach, 1989). A series of public radio and TV announcements, newspaper ads, and social media sites share literacy facts and encourage people to respond to our volunteer recruitment efforts.

Before committing, prospective volunteers are asked to commit to either one or two sessions a week for one year. Each session will last one to two hours. Tutoring is organized around "life application categories" according to the learner's readiness to learn (Smith, 1980). Adults learn best when their outcomes will contribute to their success for work and development based upon their expectations of immediate applicability. After my first student moved past Skill Book 4, I continued my literacy training to become a Tutor Trainer, Master Tutor-Literacy, and later, completed a Master's degree in Adult Education and Training.

Another great movie in the entertainment industry that illustrated some life issues that some adults experience was Stanly and Iris (Ritt, M. 1990). This movie was portrayed as a love story of a struggling widow that falls in love with an illiterate short-order cook, named Stanley, whom she teaches to read and write in her kitchen each night. Laubach materials are used throughout the movie as the tutor guided the student through the lessons and other life challenges. Stanley's project invention was an assembly line system he invented in his garage to help cool pastry products quicker, which aided in decoration, packaging, and getting the products to the customers faster and fresher. With an offer to travel to New York, Iris thought she had lost him until he returned.

CHAPTER

IV

JOB DESCRIPTION OF AN ADULT LITERACY TUTOR

"Reading for me is spending time with a friend."
– Gary Paulsen

A job description is important for any skill, task, or profession, especially for volunteer adult literacy tutors. The tutor's job description outlines the primary duties, responsibilities, and relationships between the tutor and student. Furthermore, it provides verified information related to the tutor's experience, the scope of the tutor's duties, and responsibilities that are used in the context of experience when seeking paid employment, in a related education field, if needed.

The tutor job description: Complete a 12 to 14-hour Tutor Training Workshop; Respect your student as a responsible adult.

Tutor teaches students one on one in a **confidential** setting.

Assist adult nonreaders to learn to read, improve **numeracy**, and skills for life applications.

Teach adult nonreaders the applicable life skills necessary to be productive in life and to conduct their personal affairs with confidence and pride.

Maintain student confidentiality.

Tutoring in public places, such as study rooms in public libraries or selected classrooms. Conduct initial and periodic assessments and provide improvement and goal setting, strategies and counseling.

Prepare lessons for reading, writing; and life skills as required for each student.

Conduct periodic checkups during and after each lesson.

Provide the organization director with student **information** to assist with outside placement. Complete monthly progress reports on each student's success and provides concerns as necessary for statistical reports. Beginning level, ending level, and progress level attained.

Always give positive reinforcement.

Prepare students to acquire the fifth-grade level for the GED **program** if that is their ultimate goal. The General Education Development (GED) started in 1942 as an option and viable alternative for military men who were sent overseas to fight in the war before they could complete their high school education (The History of the GED (n. d.)).

Assist adults to become self-directed, independent learners for life.

This sample statement is used when family members want information on a student not in the same household. The statement is used only after a conference with and received an agreement from my student

Sample confidentiality statement:

STATEMENT OF CONFIDENTIALITY FOR STUDENT RECORDS

Tutor; name

Student: name

Confidentiality of student records is required by federal law.

Tutor (name) will take every precaution to protect the integrity of (Student name) confidential student information. The release of ANY educational information which would identify a specific student is prohibited.

Tutor (name) may release information with a written release from the student.

In addition, due to the nature of my services, it is expected that we interact with our students with various needs from diverse backgrounds.

Tutor (name) is committed to promoting an environment in which student feels comfortable and secure. Information of a personal nature will not be disclosed to outside parties or colleagues unless it is legally required or essential to the student's progress, health, and **welfare**.

Please print the following information:

Address: _____

Phone: _____

I have read the statement above and will comply as it concerns this student.

I also understand that this form will be placed in Student (name) student record.

_____

Signature /date

Chapter

V

LIFE SKILLS

"I can accept failure. Everyone fails at something. But I cannot accept not trying."
—Michael Jordan

In addition to academic skills, life skills are important from childhood and continue throughout one's life. "Life skills are defined as any personal ability that helps an individual cope with people, problems, situations, challenges, and stressors in life. Life skills include adaptability, emotional intelligence, listening, negotiation, relationship building, and self-awareness (Medical Dictionary, 2009). During childhood, we learn how to use eating utensils, perform basic hygiene, how to clean our room, wash dishes, clean the kitchen, etc. In adulthood, those skills expand. Some teenagers learn how to assist in the kitchen; follow a basic menu, help set the table for meals for the family to eat; separate, wash laundry, and maintain the lawn.

Adults also need additional life skills including assessing and maintaining household financial transactions; preparing and maintaining a household budget; preparing a list of items needed for grocery shopping; understand the importance of **establishing** and maintaining credit. **Establish** and maintain a plan for short and long-range savings. Read, and understand instructions for products, contracts involved in purchases, financial obligations, and personal financial affairs. Reconciling their checkbook with monthly bank statements and communicating with others in, and outside of the family; accept and give constructive criticism. Reading and understanding utility bills; writing notes for self or children in school. Life skills are used inside and outside of the home, classroom, and in all life situations. Life skills training normally starts in Skill Book 3 and continues through Skill Book 4, unless the student requires a skill earlier. For example, one student needed to know how to balance their checkbook to manage finances.

CHAPTER

VI

ONE-ON-ONE TUTORING

"The secret of success is to start from scratch and keep scratching."
-Dennis Green

The one-on-one tutoring platform maintains confidentiality, is personalized, and is **focused** on tutoring one student. One-on-one tutoring keeps the student **focused** and on task. Distractors are minimized giving the student full attention to his or her lesson content. A personalized individual study plan can be developed for each student that **focuses** on their needs and successes. For example, Skill Book 3 life skills include **numeracy** skills on check writing with sample check worksheets. We progress from check writing to recording the transactions in the check register. Another worksheet is used to verify the checks that have been cleared by the bank. Finally, the last worksheet is used to balance the transactions. The balance should agree with the bank statement balance verifying any deposits and transactions not yet recorded.

Supplemental resources such as easy crossword, or easy word find puzzles help improve student-spelling skills. Recipes used from **cookbooks** expand **numeracy** skills to illustrate measurements such as cups, fractions, mixing, cooking times, and whole numbers. Sample job applications are used to provide training and highlight experience with different types of **information**. Resumes from the student's skills and cover letters assist student job seekers to prepare for and find employment. As a tutor, I maintain an outside resource list to assist the student with the interview process. For example, at the local Department of Labor employment officers services for persons with disabilities, **veterans**, and persons needing a Bond to obtain employment. Most offices offer free assistance including how to dress, makeup, and sit for the interview. Strategies **demonstrate** how to answer questions and concerns to an interview panel.

While the focus will be on reading and writing, the students have individualized lesson plans based on their needs and goals. Each student will learn life skills such as reading and understanding utility bills, writing checks, measuring quantities, reading labels, recipes, traveling directions, and making consumer purchasing decisions. At the beginning of the tutoring process, the new adult reader is taught using the pedagogy (process) approach. Over a period, the student will slowly transition toward the andragogy (adult) mode. These and other skills will be transferable from the student's workbook exercises and show the student how to apply them in everyday life.

Helping adults learn to read will help improve their quality of life for themselves and their families. Self-esteem improves knowing they can independently select items and read **information** for themselves; be able to make informed **consumer** decisions and make personal choices. Many adult non-readers face the reality of not being able to find employment, read a traffic sign, a prescription **label**, or follow simple instructions. Adult non-readers pay higher costs in purchasing products and services because they rely on product labels, thereby spending more money for their products and services. Most often choosing products with the most attractive pictures placed on rows that are waist to chest high for easier selection. They often do not seek social assistance or medical care for fear of having to complete paperwork affecting their **consumer**, medical decisions, and life choices.

Chapter

VII

HOW CAN WE UNDERSTAND THIS SITUATION?

"Stay alive by hiding between the covers of a book."
– E.B. White

There are various reasons why many adults are unable to read. According to ProLiteracy, "36 million adults in the United States cannot read, **write** nor perform basic math above the third-grade level." Some adults may have dropped out of school at an early age. Some may have struggled with a missed diagnosed reading challenge earlier in life. Some may have given up thinking the academic workload was too hard. Others may have needed to stop school to produce income to help support their family.

Regardless of the reason, literacy challenges affect every area of our lives. Many state licensing agencies still give oral exams to nonreaders to get a state driver's license. For example, New York, Virginia, South Carolina, and California to name a few provide oral or modified exams for non-readers or persons with disabilities to get a driver's license. The literacy rate in Muscogee County Georgia is seventeen percent according to the 2003 National Assessment of Adult Literacy. That means that seventeen percent of the population or approximately 2,186 persons aged 16 years and older not in school lack basic prose literacy skills and those persons cannot be tested, due to lack of understanding. This is more than an individual issue.

According to the Social Security Administration, **illiteracy** in adults is classified as a disability. The Federal Code of Regulations, 404-1564 reads, "**Illiteracy** means the inability to read or write. We consider someone illiterate if the person cannot read or write a simple message such as instructions or inventory lists even though the person can sign (write) his or her name." Generally, an illiterate person with little or no formal schooling must depend on their survival skills or enablers to living day to day.

Adult illiteracy is a personal, local, state, and national issue affecting many citizens with limited reading comprehension and coping skills. The lack of these reading, writing, and comprehension skills limits adults' ability in living and lead full enjoyable lives for themselves, their families, and they are participating in our social and political processes. Imagine not being able to read medical information in their doctor's office, completing consumer contracts to make major purchases, or writing up a shopping list for groceries.

Local newspaper content varies with the reading grade level. Most newspapers' average reading content is at the sixth grade reading level, while others are higher. For example, the Washington Post, and the USA Today newspaper average 10th grade and the New York Times average 11.8 reading grade levels (Good calculators, n. d.). An Advanced Health Care Directive for my state (Georgia) has a minimum reading grade level of 6+.

CHAPTER

VIII

MY FIRST MEMORABLE STUDENT

"If you don't like to read, you haven't found the right book."
– J.K. Rowling

O nce training was completed, I received my first assignment. To my surprise, the student lived just two doors down from me on the same street. The statistic shared in the classroom informed us that, "In 1980 the U.S. Census Bureau counted 24.3 million Americans over the age of 25 had not gone beyond the 8th grade" (New Readers Press, 1989). That means we may know someone and not recognize him or her as adult nonreaders. There may be a nonreader in someone's family and other members may not know it. Some nonreaders may have enablers that help them hide their problems. Other adults have hidden their secrets within their families for years. Nonreaders are self-conscious about others knowing they cannot read. Some nonreaders have a very strong memory that they rely upon. This is an asset for anyone, nonreader or not.

Next, I had to secure a **confidential** location for our tutoring sessions. The local library is an excellent resource and can often provide study rooms for privacy by reservation only. Since I was a soldier and lived on a military installation, I contacted our Education Center. The director gave me a room between noon and1p.m. daily since my first student was a military family member. During that time, foot traffic was low, and we were assigned a study room for our use without interruptions. I phoned my student to introduce myself and reviewed the dates and times of my availability. During our first session, introductions are exchanged, and the student's abilities were assessed and discussed. For the assessment, I used the Laubach Way to Reading Diagnostic Inventory. The students' pre-reading assessment began with a Word Inventory List. It begins with easy words such as a, it, I, my, and progresses from easy to moderate and then to more difficult words. Following the assessment, this student was placed in Skill Level 1 of the Laubach Way to Reading series.

Throughout each skill level, the student is assessed through Check-ups, Comprehension, homework, Progress Checks, and Meeting Individual Needs. Placement is reviewed, and books for the assessed Skill Level are issued as our core reading material. This level consists of the Laubach Way to Reading Skill Level 1 Student Book, and supplemental readers, In the Valley, and More Stories 1 (New Readers Press, 1986). There are four levels in this series, Skill Level 1, 2, 3, and 4. At the end of each Skill Level, the student's abilities are recorded and assessed with each final Check-up. After the results are recorded, the student is awarded a certificate for that Skill Level before proceeding to the next.

That started on a journey, now coming up on 35 years as an Adult Literacy Volunteer Tutor. Since then, I have been tutoring (teaching) adults to read, write, and improve their life skills, helping them and those that have families, feel better about themselves and improve their standard of living. The adult **learner** has needs and faces barriers that are different from those of the "traditional" student (Klein-Collins, 2011). Some needs range from a lack of opportunity, training to improve on-the-job skills, certifications for job retention in some positions, to returning to school to increase academic skills for the GED program or credentials for promotion.

In Klein-Collins' article, barriers to adult **learning** are varied and are primarily classed as time and money. My student's barrier was family in the beginning. Once the family saw the improvements, and the student's independence, their attitude slowly changed to support. That lifted my student's morale and she became more determined to **learn** as much as possible and get into a GED program to complete her high school diploma. Once I thought that age was a barrier to my education until I began seeing and reading stories of adults (50 and older) graduating from high school and college. Sharing this information with an adult nonreader gives them an incentive to want to learn and do. Learning and application have no limits!

Chapter

IX

Types of literacy

"I read a book one day and my whole life was changed."
– Orhan Pamuk

O ften, when one hears the word literacy it is used in the context of performing at grade level as a child. Non-reading adults are viewed as ignorant, not so (Garcia, A. 2013) noted in his article, that there are different forms of literacy. First, let us look at the definition of literacy. Literacy is the ability to read, write, and comprehend in your language. We must also be able to comprehend the written word, understand, and use **numeracy** skills. That is necessary for one to be functionally literate in the basics. From there, goals will lead to endless possibilities. A functionally illiterate adult cannot function on a level to adequately perform in daily life. "Adults classified as below reading level 1 may be considered functionally illiterate in the English language: i.e., unable to successfully determine the meaning of sentences, read relatively short texts, locate a single piece of **information**, or complete simple forms" (OECD 2013).

For adults age 16 and above with assessed reading level abilities that range from zero to about eighth grade will often have missed opportunities in life. The ability levels increase from grade 0 to 12th grade through school. For example, a student in third grade should be reading on a minimum of third grade reading level. "As educators today, we have seen a significant shift in what a "literate" student is. We simply cannot distinguish that simply by looks alone. There are, in fact, many other types of literacy than what we might traditionally think of." Garcia identified some areas as Digital, Computer, **Information**, Financial, Media, Technology, Political, Historical, Cultural, Multi-cultural, Document, Medical, Civics, and Visual Literacy, etc. In short, literacy, **numeracy**, and language skills are associated with every occupation, hobby, or task in our society. These subjects are not treated as equally important in the traditional definition of literacy but each is vital for the person required to possess them for success in life.

Since I have more than three decades of tutoring experience, I can safely add to this list Digital, Family, World, Financial, **Consumer**, Professional, and Biblical Literacy. Additionally, the list goes on. As we progress academically and socially, we can also see that this list continues to evolve. I can safely state that these subjects are just as important to us in today's society as in the past. For example, a driver with low literacy skills affects their ability to read a vehicle operator's manual, navigate their vehicle on streets and highways if they can't read the street names, highway markers, detour instructions, or how to read instructions to prepare their vehicle if an emergency happens.

Now place yourself in the position as a homemaker. One task of a homemaker is to prepare meals for the family, To prepare a new dish for the family, the homemaker must be able to read, understand the various sizes of baking dishes and pans. We must understand listed ingredients, whole numbers, fractions, terms like bake, broil, sauté, fry, oven, stovetop, chopped, ground, dice, peel, dried, and time to cook the dish. Additionally, we must know the difference and sizes of teaspoons, tablespoons, and cups. Finally, know the order in which to prepare and cook the ingredients for the dish.

This is one of my easy recipes:

"Big Papa's Nut Bread Recipe" (I am also known as Big Papa)

This Nut Bread Recipe is moist, sweet, and flavorful every time!

Use very ripe bananas.

Options:

- You may use unsalted peanuts, pecans, or walnuts for this recipe.
- If you are allergic to bananas, use cooked sweet potatoes.

Prep Time 15 minutes

Cook Time 50 minutes

Total Time 1 hour 5 minutes

Get all ingredients and pan/s first.

Ingredients:

¼-cup salted butter (softened at room temperature)

¼-cup canola oil

1 -cup granulated sugar

2 -whole ripe bananas mashed (or 1 cup of cooked sweet potatoes)

2 -large eggs (warmed at room temperature)

1-teaspoon vanilla flavor

1 ½- cups all self-rising flour

¼- cup buttermilk

¾- cup walnuts, peanuts, or pecans chopped (your choice)

Instructions:

Preheat oven to 325 degrees. Grease lightly, <u>one</u> large loaf pan (8 1/2" x 4 1/2" x 2 3/4" high) or <u>two</u> smaller loaf pans (8"x 33/4"x 23/8") with non-stick cooking spray and set aside. You can lightly dust with flour

In a large bowl, mix oil, butter, and sugar, stir until well combined. Stir in eggs, vanilla, banana, or sweet potatoes until smooth.

Gently stir in dry ingredients until a uniform batter has formed. Scrape sides to ensure no lumps are present. Stir in 1/2 cup of your choice walnuts, pecans, or peanuts.

LAST: add buttermilk and stir in well. Pour into prepared pan and top with remaining 1/4 cup chopped nuts. Sprinkle the top with walnuts, peanuts, or pecans.

Place the pan in the oven. Once the bread is about half cooked, cut a slit in the middle of the bread sprinkle nuts of your choice.

Bake for 50 to 60 minutes in the lower half of the oven or until completely baked. Remove from oven and cool on a cooling rack for at least 15 minutes before removing from pan. Slice and serve. The Reading Grade Level for this recipe is 4.7

That leads us into the Breakthrough to Math Series that covers four levels. After a diagnostic assessment, the student is placed on one of four levels. Level 1 covers whole number identification, adding and subtracting of whole numbers, and word problems. Level 2 covers fractions, decimals, and percent. Level 3 covers basic algebra. Level 4 covers plane geometry and volume. Two resources that I found very useful for students to use are a composition book and graph paper. After completing assignments, the composition book is an excellent resource for the student to review and study the concepts. Graph paper aids the student in understanding place value, computing numbers, number lines, and plotting angles, graphing lines, and coordinates. Both items are at most discount stores for less than five dollars.

CHAPTER

X

ADULT LEARNERS' IMMEDIATE NEEDS

"Reading one book is like eating one potato chip."
– Diane Duane

Understanding adult learners is vital in assisting them to obtain their goals. The adult learner has needs and faces barriers that are different from those of the "traditional" student (Klein-Collins). Some needs range from training to improve job skills, certification for job retention, or returning to school to increase an academic credential for promotion. Adult learners bring varied life experiences to their one on one, classroom, online, or hybrid courses. This platform combines classroom instruction with online learning and is the most promising approach for K-12 and higher education (Means et al., 2010). According to Knowles, "adult learners move from dependency toward increasing self-directness, but at different rates for different people in different dimensions of life" (Knowles, 2007). Once they decide to improve themselves through education or professional development, they must commit to finishing. That decision helps move them forward to apply and complete their intended course of instruction or become successful in learning a new skill.

"Adult learning draws upon the use of experiences as a medium of learning" (Chen, 2013). Organizing work, family activities, and school schedules are some of the challenges that adult learners contend with, in addition to parenting duties. While tutoring literacy to adult learners, some students reveal that they have various immediate needs that need attention. Normally, students begin to ask for help on issues important to them that affect their lives after they become familiar and comfortable with the tutor. One way to address their fear and doubt is to review the strengths they currently possess. "I can …, I have …, I know how-to, etc. Tutors can assist in addressing issues needed to move forward, helping the student understand progress will move them closer to their goal of independence. Additionally, adult learners' self-assessment helps them realize what they need to perform skills, occupations, or activities.

One example, a student wanted to know how to properly prepare and understand what is required to file income taxes having never done it before since working. For this request, I opened my list of outside resources and gave them the contact number for a local organization that assists low-income households free of charge to prepare their income taxes. These outside resources will be covered later. I added two sessions to cover the IRS Form 1040 (1999) with the student and spouse. The form has subtle changes every year. The form for 1999 has 69 line items to review and consider. The 2020 form has 38-line items and a new Third Party designation for a "Power of Attorney" if desired along with a question concerning virtual currency.

In addition to improving reading and writing skills, the adults' **numeracy** and Math skills are assessed. The assessment results help gauge the students' starting point. Some students' immediate needs include improving money management skills. Basic Math skills needed are adding, subtraction, multiplication, and division. The use of writing number words such as whole numbers, decimals, fractions, and percents, is needed in writing checks. Additionally, signing your name requires cursive writing. For example, skills to write checks, including maintaining a check register, balancing a checkbook, and preparing a household budget are some of the skills needed to manage a household and personal finances. Examples are used to help the student understand and progress through the steps to complete the family management processes. Personal assistance, if requested, is scheduled and provided for their private **information**.

CHAPTER

XI

SOME ISSUES THAT CAN HAMPER ADULT LEARNING

"Today a reader, tomorrow a leader."
– Margaret Fuller

Some barriers for adult learners often start with themselves. Pride and fear of others finding out they cannot read are embarrassing for many of us as adults. Others range from some side effects of some **medicine**, a lack of adequate income, needing shelter, no utilities at home, lack of childcare, or no transportation. As tutors, we must learn and understand our students, be observant of their needs, and observe mannerisms that present clues of the students' actions. One of my students wore glasses; however, in this instance, he kept adjusting his focus by looking over the lenses, leaning closer, or pulling further away from the text while reading. When I inquired about his glasses giving him problems, he stated that he bought them at a discount store. Several weeks later, my student arrives with new glasses. He said, "I can see everything now, my doctor made new ones for me". Progress improved from that point forward.

Some adults think that their age is a barrier to learning and improving their life. I once thought that my age was a barrier and put off perusing a degree. Afterward, I began reading articles and seeing celebratory clips on television of adults over the age of fifty completing high school and college, I changed my mind and began preparing myself through reading and researching degrees to help myself and others. As learning options expanded to online platforms, opportunities opened up to many adults including myself to continue my degree. The financial barrier is also a challenge for many students. Some adults often let educational opportunities pass because of funding deficits and a lack of resources.

Another issue that can hamper learning is a lack of funds for the student to pay for their books. These books cost less than ten dollars. Many employers offer tuition assistance as a benefit of full-time employment. Due to our current employment situation, some businesses like Walmart and Target also offer tuition to part-time employees. Others may offer tuition reimbursement. There are free online courses in academic and certification courses. Besides, some prescribed medications may affect the students' performance. Unless revealed to you, some medications can impair comprehension and aggravate the students' memory. Often, when I pick up prescriptions from my Pharmacist, he or she normally gives me a counseling information sheet for the medication. Most of us do not read them. They are very important. Those sheets provide information on the medication, its use, and how to use it. More importantly, some side effects and drug interactions, and how to treat possible overdoses are important for all of us. It is important to read the medication information before taking the prescribed medication. Armon (2010) in his article, Caution! These 10 Drugs Can Cause Memory Loss states that "For a long time doctors dismissed forgetfulness and mental confusion as a normal part of aging." Some medications can impair our concentration; make us feel tired, sleepy, and irritable, regardless of age. Again, the prescription information, precautions, and medical side effects. Look it up or confer with your pharmacist or physician. I have purchased skill books for several students that could not afford them. I will purchase and give them the book and tell them, "This is my investment in you."

Another challenge that can hamper learning in adults has misdiagnosed symptoms called dysgraphia and dyslexia. Dysgraphia is a disability that affects fine motor skills in the hands that affect handwriting or tying a shoelace for example (Frye, D. n. d.). For adult nonreaders, other symptoms emerge as mixing upper and lower case letters or print and cursive letters. These symptoms also show up as simple spelling errors and the student often prefers oral rather than written instruction. Unless revealed or the tutor picks up patterns during their tutoring sessions, these symptoms will continue to be unrecognized.

Dyslexia is called a reading disability that affects areas of the brain that process language. That involves difficulty reading due to problems identifying speech sounds and learning how they relate to letters and words (decoding) (DSM-5, 2013). Emotional support also plays an important role. Though there's no cure for dyslexia, early assessment and intervention result in the best outcome. Sometimes dyslexia go undiagnosed in children for years and isn't recognized until adulthood, but it's never too late to seek help.

Rapid changes in technology often challenge adult nonreaders to learn new skills or impede their progress. These range from digital appliances, like ovens, microwaves, newer model refrigerators, television sets with digital remote controls, and texting on cell phones, setting a digital calendar, clock, entering and saving contacts on computers, cell phones, computer functions, touch screens in automobiles, and performing other digital functions. Other challenges may include online banking, paying bills, and transferring funds from one account to another. Online financial functions may include filing individual income tax returns and purchases from one's favorite retailer.

Sometimes a new adult learner experiences negative comments from within their household. Comments like, "Why do you want to learn to read now at your age?" That drains the students' motivation to learn. When I see the expressions on their face and know this session may not go well until we address these issues. On the other hand, positive comments from family members are great morale boosters for the emerging readers' morale because they feel supported at home.

Chapter

XII

Individual study plan

"Reading is a basic tool in the living of a good life."
– Mortimer J. Adler

An individual study plan helps each student succeed. Separate study plans for each student with defined goals are different and fluid. The study plans help keep the student-**focused**, see their continuing progress at each level, and highlight areas that need improvement. After Skill Book 2, the tutor can set up a student's study plan based on their needs and goals. Some students just want to learn to read. Others may want to get into adult education classes, acquire their GED, move on to technical schools, college, or seek remediation in their occupational area of need. Skills such as simple reading, phonics, and vowel sounds are taught during our twice-weekly sessions of two hours each.

Improving basic literacy skills enhances every area of one's life, from personal, social, home, professional, and the community. Adults that are devoid of these skills place additional challenges on the daily demands of their technical skills to compete in our digital era. One way to help improve our students' progress is by identifying their areas of interest. For example, if a students' interest is a skill, profession, or hobby, create a word list for learning, review, and application. A plumber, for example, must know several hundred words and phrases associated with that profession. Drainpipe, water pressure, valve plug, threads, quote, and certification just to name a few. Additionally, a plumber must be proficient and certified to install items such as water heaters, septic systems, sewers, faucets, drainage systems, and air conditioning units to install and make repairs. Think of a hobby or skill that you like. A word list can be created to give the student more confidence in that hobby or skill as you build knowledge. For example, the game of Chess has about 500 words associated with it from the board, each space, piece, has a name, and moves with the object to win the game.

Reviewing the student's needs and goals provide a visual for them to see and chart their progress. A study plan is a fluid plan and can be developed using a calendar, note pad, or a computer. For example, a writing assignment with a targeted due date of two weeks from today means the student must schedule a time to research our subject, write a rough draft, first paper, revise and rewrite, verify sources and complete the final write-up and turn it in on or before the deadline. Based on your life schedule, adequate time must be set aside for each step of the process to ensure your success. After the tutor reviews the assignment, the student can read the notes, revise the assignment, and keep it for future reference. Every assessment along the way informs the student of their successes and areas that need improvement to develop strategies for continuing their learning journey.

Each study plan starts with the basic literacy curriculum that adds additional information and resources for each student as needed. Maintaining a word list builds vocabulary, spelling, and phonics skills. Most students ask for assistance if needed to acquire new information, improve job skills, and prepare for promotion and signing documents. Cursive writing is discussed in the next chapter. This is the level students learn how to hold their writing instruments, practice penmanship, and improve handwriting skills.

Chapter

XIII

Cursive writing

"Handwriting is the garden of the sciences."
— Abu Dulaf

Skill Book 3 is the level the student learns or improves their cursive writing skills. In Lessons 22 through 24, the student learns to write small and capital letters in cursive. Cursive writing is a system of forming and connecting letters to form words and sentences. This form of penmanship becomes your handwriting style. Once perfected, homework and lessons are written in cursive. The tutor helps the student open their mind to see other possibilities while improving in their selected areas of need through journaling. Journaling is a way of improving writing skills while writing about oneself and plans, or how they feel from one day's activities to the next. Writing daily helps, the student think about those plans to reach their set goal. Again, a composition book is an excellent resource the student can use for this exercise.

Graphologists have been studying the link between behavior and handwriting since the days of Confucius in 500 BC when he warned us all to avoid "a man whose writing sways like a reed in the wind (Gonor, A. 2019)." New research shows that learning cursive (writing) will improve reading speed and train the brain to have better hand-eye coordination (Knowles, 2015). Have you been complimented on your handwriting? As cursive writing improves, so does personal writing style, comprehension, and pride. Your signature is still required on important financial and legal and medical documents. Your handwriting may be compared to a signature on official documents, such as ID cards, your driver's license, or other forms of identification. Digital signatures are sometimes used for some electronic documents. If an adult cannot write, he or she may be allowed to sign their name by making an X, and someone else must witness their X by signing their name to authenticate the X as the person's genuine signature.

Some handwriting analysts also study writing samples to determine personality types. A thank-you note, letter, or a handwritten birthday or greeting card in your handwriting sets you apart. Many people still cherish a handwritten letter today. Most handwritten cards and letters are saved as keepsakes and read again later. For that, I am guilty. Cursive writing can also be useful in comparing the current and past writing assignments in journals. Note: Get a pencil and pen that fits your student's hand comfortably and encourage them to practice, practice and practice.

A comfortable writing instrument is vital. Select a pen or pencil that comfortably fits your writing hand. Some new writers may benefit from using pen or pencil grips used to aid in writing stability. First use lined paper to model the cursive alphabet. Then challenge yourself by writing the alphabet as one continuous stream. Finally, go back to cross the letters t, x, and dot the letter i and j. As your **penmanship** style improves so will the unique writing style that you have created.

Chapter
XIV

COMMUNITY RESOURCES TO ASSIST NEW ADULT READERS

*"The more that you read, the more things you will know.
The more that you learn the more places you'll go."*

-Dr. Seuss

Once the student becomes comfortable with their tutor, they often ask for the tutor's assistance or recommendation during their sessions on various issues. I compiled a contact list of social service organizations in the community to aid my students. Helping a student get access to needed resources also improves the student's morale, motivation, and independence. Some social service organizations that are on my list include the United Way, Salvation Army, Red Cross, Local Food Bank, local Department of Labor, and others. With this list, I made a contact sheet containing the organization's points of contact, phone number, address, hours of operation, services provided, and requirements to obtain services. The United Way also has a national number, 211 to call from anywhere for assistance.

Outside resources and activities also help improve our students' life skills from Skill Book 3, 4, and forward through activities that are necessary to assist and expand their knowledge and independence in life. Some of these resources are listed in the Skill Books along with Financial

Literacy sessions. Some banks gladly provide handouts on checkbook registers, information on how to manage various types of accounts, and how to save and manage funds.

(1). Use a monthly calendar to improve knowledge of learning the days of the week, months of the year, schedule appointments, log study time, and review spelling and content knowledge. Using a yearly calendar is a great resource. Many calendars may be purchased for as low as one dollar at various discount stores.

(2). Cell phone and computer skills are improved after the student has learned the alphabet, writing, and spelling comprehension. Being able to text requires another language skill and typing mostly with your thumbs while holding the phone rather than your fingers as used on a full computer keyboard. Newer smartphones have a microphone app where you touch it and speak. Verify the content before sending the message. Some words may be misunderstood or misspelled confusing the receiver or displaying an unintended message.

(3). **Establishing** a budget to fit household, expense needs, and debt management

(4). Review and understand simple contracts

(5). Writing a note or a letter for various reasons

(6). Learn to use the city, state, and national map to find locations and route directions. Some newer model cars are equipped with navigation/ map directions for easy route locations. Also, smartphones contain maps to display maps, navigation, and the location of destinations.

(7). Review various newspapers for interesting articles, i.e. Obituary columns and topics of the student's interest,

(8). Review the applicable state driver's handbook.

(9). Improving cursive writing skills are required for writing letters cards, signing important contracts, checks, and other legal documents. For non-writing adults that make their mark with an X or another symbol, a witness is often required to complete transactions.

(10). Understand the importance and purpose of savings, taxes, and various types of **insurance,** i.e., home or rental, auto, health, and life.

(11). Learn to start a business and purchase a home if that is their goal.

(12). Learn the importance and purpose of maintaining good credit.

One of the best resources that can assist a new reader is a cassette recorder/ player with headphones. To assist the learners, the tutor reads the lesson chart words and stories into the unit. The student can listen and read along helping improve sight word recognition, pronunciation, and reading comprehension skills. The strategy is to read smoothly and a little faster than the student currently reads. As the student listens to the recordings. They are instructed to read aloud following the printed text. Once they are comfortable reading the text independently and assessed they move to the next assignment. The local public library is an excellent resource to find adult content material for low-level readers. Most libraries have grade-level books in special sections. Just ask.

The book, Horton Hatches the Egg (Seuss, 1940), K-4th grade level, became one of my favorite books. It has adult content that low-level readers can understand and share with their children. Once I was relaxing, I read it alone and got a completely different perspective. From the adult view, it tells the story of a single mother wanting to get some respite from her (egg) child. She (Mayzie) asked her neighbor, Horton the elephant to watch her child for a while. Horton was honest, dependable, and friendly. He accepted the responsibility and Mayzie went on vacation. Horton took such great care of the egg that when it hatched, surprise, it looked just like Horton, except for its two big floppy ears. Meanwhile, Mayzie was relaxing on the beach down south. While relaxing on the beach, she saw Horton and her baby. Child services got involved and Horton was granted full custody of the child after they went to court. That is heavy, even for a child to comprehend. There are many other children's books with adult content, easy reading, and enjoyable.

The best tutoring resource in the community is the public library. My students worked during the week so our reservations for the study room were reserved and met for sessions every Saturday, two hours for twelve years until the pandemic hit and put us out of business. The meeting rooms are private and provide everything needed, including a table, whiteboard, chairs, and privacy. As knowledge and application improve, the new learner can sign for and get their library card, tour all library resources, and learn keyboarding skills, research careers, and academic goals. Our local public library provides an assortment of low-level reading materials of high interest for adults.

These High Interest – Low-Level Reading titles normally start about the second-grade level and progress upward. The librarian can also assist in helping new readers assess the reading grade level of local and national newspapers. Categories include sports, fiction, magazines, science, politics, history, and others. For example, the USA Today newspaper ranges from ninth to tenth-grade reading level. The Atlanta Journal-Constitution newspaper averages an eighth-grade reading level. Some articles in various publications are written at a higher reading level and some are written at a lower level. Using the Flesch-Kincaid method of calculating the reading grade level (Fleming, 2019) is an excellent resource to assist the student to obtain the material of their interest.

Chapter

XV

My Second Memorable Student

"One way to make the world better is by improving yourself."

– Wilkie Williams

During my assignment at Fort Stewart, GA, I founded the Liberty County Literacy Council in early 1994. The word started spreading throughout the community. In September 1994, Ms. Margaret Hendrix a correspondent of the Coastal Courier newspaper interviewed me. The subject was entitled "Everyone Can Learn." During that interview, I stated, "Potential adult students need to know that lessons are one on one, private, and confidential. There is no need for embarrassment or hesitancy." Students learning the basics of literacy do not work well in-group settings. It is hard for some adults to come forward and ask for help and many may never ask for assistance if they believe they will be placed into group settings and peers in their class may make their situation public.

My second memorable student was over 73 years of age. At this point, he was retired from being a laborer in the construction industry. During our assessment session, I learned that he wanted to learn to read and better understand the Bible. At the end of our first session, he asked,

"What will I have to pay for these classes?" When I told him, it would be no cost, just pay for your workbook, which is about ten dollars if you can afford it, otherwise, it is free. He replied, "I can afford that cost, and it is not a problem at all." In the second session, he brought his Bible along with his workbook. I informed him that after we complete Skill Book 1, we would do our basic work first and set aside 15 minutes for reading and studying the Bible during each successive session.

During our tutor training, we also learned how to assess the reading grade levels with various materials that are of interest to our students (Feinberg, M. 2010). According to Fienberg, "The King James Version" of the Bible (KJV) averages the 12th-grade reading level. Some different versions of the Bible are less, and some are higher. The easiest Bible to read is the "New Century Version" (NCV) 3rd grade and the "New International Version" (NIV) which is assessed at the 8th-grade reading level." After our second session, I introduced my student to a large print edition of the KJV Bible, which he preferred. Reading was easier moving forward. The next issue was finding a Greek and Hebrew Dictionary to assist with definitions. After searching for a couple of weeks I found a Strong's Exhaustive Concordance of the Bible that also contains a Greek and Hebrew Dictionary. The cost was prohibitive for my student, so I used it for our sessions and added it to my library. I currently own and use one for tutoring, my readings, and studies to this day. Developing a study plan for this student was an enjoyable task. The concordance proved to be a valuable resource and an excellent tool to track the student's reading and writing progress.

As the student's interest picked up, I found a new resource to aid in finding grade lever books for reading enjoyment. Find A Book, (n. d.) aids the readers with the reading grade level of published works by subject and author. One book chosen by the student was Uncle Tom's Cabin by Harriet Beecher Stowe. This was above the student's level of 11 to 12th grade, however, since the subject was interesting, I set aside twenty minutes of our two-hour sessions and we read portions of it together. As my student's reading improved, I could see the changing facial expressions of appreciation and new pride just beaming from ear to ear.

CHAPTER

XVI

MOTIVATING THE ADULT STUDENT TO BE A SELF-DIRECTED LEARNER

"Reading for me is spending time with a friend."
– Gary Paulsen

Often the self-directed learner believes he/ she cannot learn to read. Once an adult decides to learn, move pride aside, their outlook on life and goals began to change. Internal motivation is the drive to do better for oneself and your family. As they learn to improve their literacy skills in this situation, they become self-directed learners (SDL) (Segen's Medical Dictionary, 2011). The main characteristic of self-directed learning is the degree to which the learner maintains control over their learning and includes the learner's personality, ownership, motivation, internal drive, and willingness to succeed. SDL is a process in which a student is responsible for organizing and managing his or her learning activities and needs. SDL encourages individuals to become responsible for their learning, identify gaps in their knowledge, and critically appraise new **information**.

Once the adult learner asks for help with improving their literacy skills, they have to overcome one of their biggest hurdles, pride. Self-directed learners are responsible for what and when they learn. Once the learner realizes his or her goal is possible their learning begins. The learner acknowledges this is possible and initiates the learning process. Knowles (1975) stated, "People who take the initiative in learning, learn more things better than people who sit in the classroom." External motivation from the tutor aids the internal motivation of the student as they move through the learning process.

One strategy a tutor can take is to assess their student's learning styles. Learning styles guide the way we learn. They also change the way we internally represent experiences, the way we recall information, and even the words we choose. The most assessed learning styles for adult learners are visual, verbal, and aural. With the visual style, we see the information and relate to it by explaining a picture in a book or a mural. The aural style enables us to hear and relate to the information after listening to a recorded presentation. The verbal style lets us speak and relate to the discussed content in a dialog discussion.

Another useful technique for assisting learners is duet reading. For this strategy, the tutor selects a story or passage with which the student is familiar. The tutor and the student read together. The tutor reads smoothly and at a normal pace just slightly faster than the student does. This is called the duet or paired reading, a technique that allows tutors to vary the amount of support provided to the student while reading aloud together. Make it more interesting by allowing the student to choose the content. Duet reading aids in student comprehension, fluency, and confidence while improving their morale. They continue to improve and increase reading as they progress through each grade level. Compare this to singing a song together.

CHAPTER

XVII

STRATEGIES TO IMPROVE READING COMPREHENSION

"If you don't like to read, you haven't found the right book."
– J.K. Rowling

As I mentioned earlier, being able to travel the world and explore new interests from turning the pages of a good book opens the reader to new exciting possibilities. Aldous Huxley wrote, "Every man who knows how to read has in his power to magnify himself, to make his life fully significant and interesting" (Huxley, n. d.). Improving reading comprehension is not a one-task approach. The learner must improve their spelling, phonics, writing, and vocabulary skills, which require word knowledge and being able to determine meanings of words in context as part of a sentence. This helps improve prior knowledge, experience, apply current skills and boost intelligence.

One strategy to aid in word recognition is to use Word Find or Word Search puzzle books. These books are available at most local discount stores for one dollar each. They aid in word recognition and spelling improvement. Another skill to improve is context clues; determining meanings of word clues in surrounding words in sentences as you read. Crossword puzzles are excellent for helping improve definition and spelling skills. A health benefit for adults is improving cognitive ability. Doing so helps one understand the **information** that they read. The Alzheimer's Association recommends working crossword puzzles to help stave off dementia. "Reading, writing, doing crossword puzzles, and solving challenging puzzles may help lower risk of Alzheimer's disease. Now a new study shows how mental stimulation may help protect the brain" (Landau, et. al, 2012). Crossword puzzles are available in various skill levels from easy to expert. Start with an easy puzzle and graduate up to harder levels as you succeed.

Another reading strategy is reading aloud. Reading aloud helps you understand, hear as you pronounce words, and listen to your voice inflections as you read. Reading aloud helps enhance speaking skills and fluency. Listening as you speak the content also helps with decoding skills. Timing is improved to enhance speech delivery skills. "Providing a minimum of 15 to 30 minutes each day for independent reading is vital to help students improve reading fluency, accuracy, comprehension, and increase their vocabulary" (Bales, K, 2018). This practice benefits any age group that is learning to improve their reading skills. Duet reading is a process where a reader reads with a nonreader. Help the nonreader choose a book or article that is within their reading interest level. The tutor and student read aloud; the tutor reads a little faster and smoother than the student does. This helps the slow reader build comprehension, speed, and confidence. This exercise is like you teaching a young reader and the learning experience is just as enjoyable.

Establishing a reading log is an excellent way to record reading activities. Keeping a reading log aids comprehension. This is done with a favorite book, newspaper article, or magazine. I find that keeping a reading log also helps improve comprehension and recall what I read. For beginning readers, fifteen to thirty minutes a day is a good start. As comprehension improves, the reading period can be lengthened up to one hour. Maintaining a list of words that can be looked up in the dictionary for pronunciation and definitions also aids spelling improvement. A reading log is an excellent way of keeping track of your reading over time and being able to list the books that you have read. For example, **label** a sheet of paper; Reading Log. Write the date, name of the book or article, list the number of pages read, and the time (15 to 30 minutes). This is great for new and emerging readers.

Emerging readers that use word lists for various tasks and professional careers continue to rise in their chosen pursuit. Webb and Dang published on Essential Word Lists (2016) that contains 176 words for beginning / emerging readers. Maintaining a list of words from reading various readings is an invaluable way to help improvise one's vocabulary as new reading adults move from functional to literate. A non-reading adult rarely comparison shops, pays more for goods often based upon the visual images in advertising in stores, on shelves, billboards, and television. For example, a Dolch Sight Word List for Kindergarten students starts with 100 basic words. In the 12th grade, the list contains 100 hard spelling words. Academic word lists for most professions exceed 2000 words. A collegiate word list can exceed 5000 words.

With the advent of Smartphones, we can use apps to listen to and read some of our favorite books and the Bible. Some devices allow the use of the microphone tab to speak, compose and send messages. These devices allow weak readers and writers to communicate with family and friends. Depending on the speakers' voice inflection and pronunciation sometimes garbles their message.

CHAPTER

XVIII

SOME TECHNOLOGY CHALLENGES FOR THE NON-READING ADULT LEARNER

"I don't care where you come from; I want to know where you are going."

– Andrew Young

Technology challenges for the beginning adult learner provide unique issues. These challenges range from not being able to use computers and other devices for **information** and learning new skills. Students at levels 0-1 will have unique challenges with sentence structure and understanding content. One resource that I use is a large-size keyboard for our students to practice, identifying and finding letters with their fingers. As these skills improve, students can transfer those skills to email, smartphones with texting apps, paying for purchases, using debit or credit cards to complete applications, and transacting personal and professional business on the internet. "Thirty-three percent of low-skilled working adults are White, 21 percent are Black, 39 percent are Hispanics, and eight percent are other ethnicities" (OCED, 2013). Low-level reading adults have difficulty in writing letters, submitting employment applications, or completing resumes online.

For example, one of my students could recite the letters in their name but could not identify the letters of their name when placed in front of them in random order. In this instance, technology would be an obstacle until the student's alphabetical knowledge, writing, and spelling skills are improved. In addition to the Skill Book 1 lessons, I drew a replica of a computer keyboard. This proved to be a great tool to help my student identify the capital and small letters of the alphabet out of sequence. Once the student applies the knowledge to identify and find the letters on the keyboard confidence improves. These skills are then applied to the computer where the student learns to start building keyboarding skills, to type words, sentences and apply **duet**-reading technics to build confidence on the keyboard.

Some older students today may not welcome mobile devices used for texting, mobile banking applications nor have experience with them. If these skills are required as part of their employment, they now have another challenge to learn various business devices and learn their applications to perform tasks to continue their employment. Once the student reveals needed instruction on a situation, the tutors acquire resources, prepare future sessions for training and add them as part of the lesson along with assigned homework. Some new cell phones have a microphone icon that allows one to tap the icon and then speak. This is an invaluable aid to a none- reader or weak reader to speak their messages. Preparations are made to include new tasks in the student's study plan. As a result, a 15 to 30-minute block of instruction can be used in each two-hour session to help the student learn those skills needed for their personal and professional progress.

CHAPTER

XIX

ASSESSING STUDENT PROGRESS

"I could spend the rest of my life reading, just satisfying my curiosity."

– Malcolm X

After each Skill Book, students are assessed on their progress. The assessments are materials designed for each level to test student knowledge, competency, and progress. "Materials-based assessments refer to the practice of evaluating learners based on tests following completion of a particular set of curriculum materials" (Imel, 1990). Measuring student progress is vital during our counseling sessions. The goal is to ensure the student understands that these sessions are to help improve their reading proficiency comprehension and life skills.

During our **confidential** counseling sessions, I open with the assessment from our last session. Next, we review the current assessment, highlight academic progress, and discuss activities involved in the next skill level. The student's informal needs are assessed based on their requests, job requirements if any, or life skills needs. Handwriting, including penmanship and cursive writing, is continually assessed. As an example, if budgeting and personal finances were an issue, we discuss total income by asking does your total net income meet your current total expenses? Net income is the amount received after taxes and other deductions. The question can be answered without providing actual figures unless the student wants and requests help with computations. Next, we discuss any areas that need modification and why to ensure progress. Any computations are given to the student, none are retained by the tutor.

Does your student need more assistance? To help keep my student-focused and on track, we can contact a social service organization to get our student a referral or find one by calling 211. By checking the initial interview notes, we know if the student wears glasses. I can simply ask if he /she is satisfied with their current prescription for their glasses. Always close on a positive note and offer help or refer the student for assistance if needed. These **confidential** sessions follow a simple format throughout their stay in the program.

Thus, my purpose is to assist the student in elevating their whole self to improve their total outcomes. If the adult learner and tutor have sessions of one hour a day for five days a week, the grade change would take almost two months. Two hours of study each week takes about five months to reach that point. "Each session involves a sound-reading chart, an associated story, writing lesson, review, and homework" (Laubach et. al., 2011). Regular assessments show the progress made and the tutor can adjust lessons as needed to keep the adult learner focused and on track to continue their academic, and life skills improvement. As the student progresses through the learning sessions some of the techniques used may seem juvenile, however, the method of learning gets them from the point of assessment to achieving their goal. Proud moments come when the student affirms, "Yes, I did it!" That smile and look of confidence are more rewarding than two stacks of cash. One student always wanted to take a photo of their completion certificate for each skill level. I made it a grand event each time. After level 4, we ate a cone at his favorite local ice cream shop. I was just as happy as my student for their progress, determination to improve their outcome, and self-esteem. My reward is seeing a student achieve their level of competency and skills to move forward towards their goal.

CHAPTER

XX

MOVING FORWARD

"The successful man will look for work even after he has found a job."
– Joshua I. Smith

By now, you have realized that teaching an adult to read and write is a rewarding experience. Unlike working with a group of students, tutoring one on one, we can assess the student's progress and map improvement strategies of skills that the student needs to improve their skills and goals for the future. We may incorporate new materials needed to move the student towards their intended reading or professional goal. One experience is to write about themselves and share their life experiences in their journal. This provides an opportunity for the student to read their work, correct errors and improve vocabulary, move to other projects and see their progress. Completing the Literacy Program enables one to explore the world, visualize new possibilities beyond the basics, move into a GED program and improve their outlook on life.

After Skill Book 4 and passing the TABE test, the student can move into Adult Basic Education (ABE) classes. The TABE is the assessment Test of ABE and is used to determine a student's placement level for entry into a General Education Development (GED) program. The five levels of assessment include:

L Literacy	limited literacy and assesses non-readers up to first grade (0 - 1st)
E Easy	easy and assesses second to fourth grade (2nd – 4th
M Medium	medium and assesses fourth to sixth grade (4th – 6th)
D Difficult	difficult and assesses sixth through ninth grade (6th - 9th)
A Advanced	advanced and assesses ninth through twelfth grade plus (9th - 12+)

Students taking the test have three hours to complete 195 questions. Students may choose between paper or computer tests. After completing the TABE test, students can move into ABE classes and work to earn their high school diploma. Today, there are options for adults to earn certification in skills for employment that do not require a degree or a high school diploma. Some technical colleges depending on the location and needed occupations or needed occupations in the area offer such certifications as, Nurse Aide, Pastry Specialist, Preparation Cook, Welding, Forklift Operator, Painter, Auto Mechanic, and others.

All occupations can be researched in alphabetical order from A-Z, or occupation of interest. According to this free government website, www.mynextmove.org, these occupations list pay ranges from $23,730 to 28,540 and above. Tutors can help their students by checking the technical colleges in their area so that the student can decide the career interest and the route to take. They can improve required skills for their choice of profession, and move forward. Another site is the Occupational Outlook Handbook www.bls.gov/ooh. Reading about their chosen careers and professions of interest may be researched by career title, salary, certification, education level and offers insight into what the student should expect to know about their career choices and the number of jobs available by region. For example, Entry-level positions such as Cashiers must know mathematics, make the change, process credit, and debit cards, count change and keep track of the money in their registers and be able to stand for long periods.

CHAPTER

XXI

RECORDKEEPING

"Whatever you have learned or received or heard from me or seen in me—put it into practice. And the God of peace will be with you."

-Philippians 4:9

Finally, one of the most important tasks for a tutor and the literacy organization is good recordkeeping. The tutor must keep good records of each student's sessions, including tutoring hours, preparation and travel, any outside services, or any agency referrals that assisted the student during the month. After each checkup is completed, the student receives a diploma for that skill level with their name on it. Then they can move to the next skill level. The organization must also keep track of service hours to the community, attendance, demographics, and the number of people served in the community. This **information** also provides helpful data when applying for grants and soliciting donations from individuals and organizations. I keep on each student including the Initial Learning Assessment, the Monthly Attendance, Periodic Learning Assessment, and Learning Goals. The Monthly Attendance is important to the tutor for listing dates of attendance, lessons covered, hours, preparation for lessons, total monthly hours, any referrals to agencies for assistance outside of tutoring are listed. At the end of the month, this information is forwarded to the organization's director.

The Periodic Learning Assessment contains the student's contact information, goals, and the results of the initial assessment, monthly progress, observations, and skills improvement. This continuous assessment is updated monthly and maintained by the tutor until the student moves into a General Educational Development Program (GED). This program was developed in 1942 as an alternative for military men who were sent overseas to fight in the war before completing their high school education. It has since grown to serve as a pathway to the high school equivalency for civilians. Today, many entry-level employment positions request that a potential employee have at least a high school diploma or a GED certificate. The tutor keeps records of the student's goals; start dates, progress, and completion dates until the student leaves the program, then it goes into the student's record with the program director. A student must pass a comprehension test at the fifth-grade level to be eligible for entry into the GED program if that is their desire towards a goal.

Conclusion

"Education must not simply teach work … it must teach life."

– W. E. B. Du Bois

According to data from the 2014 U.S. Census Bureau, statistics indicate that 19 percent of English-speaking adults cannot read a newspaper, much less complete a job application. That places those adults at risk of overpaying for goods, services, and not being able to provide for themselves or their families. Statistics also tell us that there are more adult nonreaders today than were identified in the 1980 census. The benefit of being empowered to live a full life, able to be self-sufficient; expanding one's dreams, and setting realistic goals for the new adult reader and their family's future empowers the whole household. The triple joy comes as an adult can read with their young school-age children and be able to function independently.

On the job, the new reader can perform his or her tasks with more pride. Throughout my 35 years as a volunteer tutor, I have never thought that I should have done something else. That is my calling as a volunteer tutor. My efforts have made a difference in each adult that I had the opportunity and privilege to tutor through each skill level in our program. Adult learners made a tremendous improvement in their reading and their family's life. Possibilities for each new adult reader emerge as their options expand for future growth. A completion and presentation certificate is awarded to the new reader as their accomplishment and priceless as one would receive for their graduation of various endeavors. The confirmation comes with a "thank you" after our sessions and sometimes a chance meeting in the community. Comments such as, "Thanks for helping me, I feel better already." "I am going to make it and reach my goal."

Appendix 1. Sample Check 1.

https://inet.chia.state.ma.us/epayments/helpfiles/HelpImages/check_sample.gif

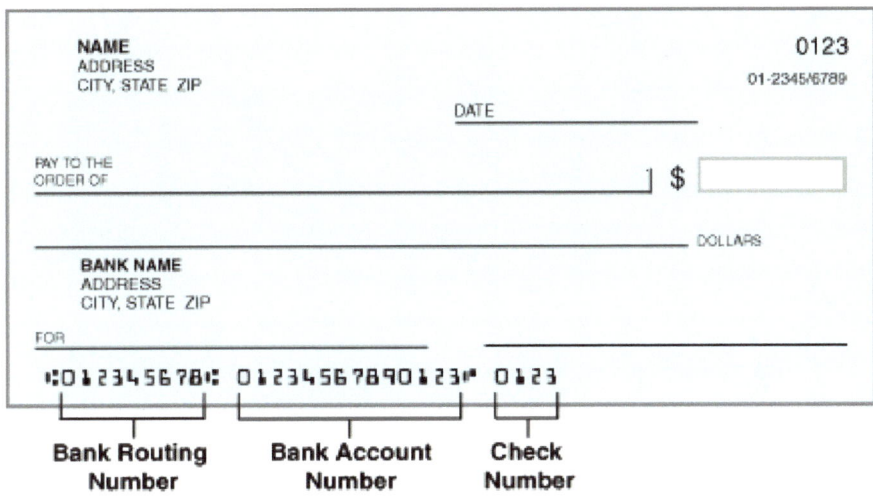

Appendix 1. Sample Check 2.

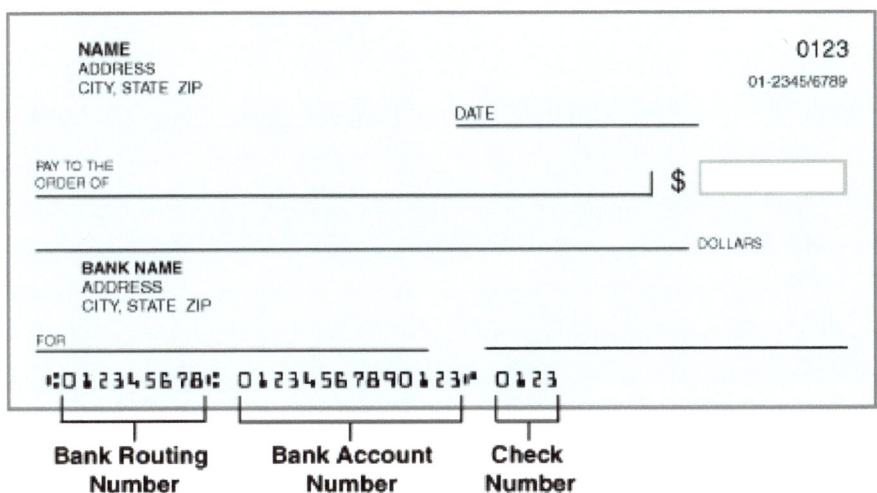

Appendix 2. Sample Check Register 1.

https://www.printablepaper.net/samples/CheckRegister.png

Number	Date	Transaction	Withdrawal	√	Deposit	$	

Appendix 3. Article from The Coastal Courier, dated. Sept. 11, 1994

'Everyone can learn'

Literacy council head in battle for everyone's self-esteem.

By Margaret Hendrix
Courier Correspondent

The old man was 73 years old, had worked all his life and raised a family. Now he had one dream. He wanted to learn to read. Then he could read God's holy word for himself — could read and understand the Bible. He needed help.

SGM David J. Boyce, Jr.was there. He taught the old man, who ended up reading not only English, but Greek and Hebrew from the Bible, also. It was one of Boyce's most memorable times as a tutor for the National Literacy Council.

It is success stories such as this that keep Boyce going — and the thanks. Students are so grateful.

"I always know they've learned something when they say 'Thank You,'" Boyce said.

Thousands can't read

Boyce knows that there are people just like that old man in Liberty County. Liberty County has thousands of functionally illiterate adults.

Some people think that any adult who can't read is either lazy or dumb. This is not so. People who are illiterate may function well in society. Boyce said there are many reasons why adults have not learned.

"There may have been social issues within the family circle," Boyce says. "The student might have needed to go to work to support the family. Also, some students may have been overlooked in school because teachers can't give one-on-one attention all the time. Some people don't learn well in groups."

Photo by Margaret Hendrix
LIBRARY USE — David Boyce, organizer of the Liberty County Literacy Council returns some materials to the Liberty County Library on Memorial Drive in Hinesville.

GLOSSARY

A

Academic: General or liberal studies minus technical or vocational education.

Adult: Anyone over the age of sixteen and not in school.

Announcement: A message given by voice or in writing.

B

Benefits: Support received from work or learning.

C

Comprehension: Capable of understanding the written or verbal word.

Confidential: Information told to a trusted person that will not tell anyone else.

Consumer: Any person that buys and uses products and services.

Cookbook: A book or collection of recipes that provides directions for preparation, uses, and consumption (eating).

Cursive: Individual penmanship in which letters are joined forming written words.

D

Deductions: Subtracting necessary expenses from the whole amount of legal income.

Demonstrate: A process that shows how things are performed in order.

Donor(s): A person that gives money to help fund a literacy organization.

Duet: Tutor and student reading the same lines together.

E

Enabler: Someone that assists a nonreader to perform tasks without criticism.

Establish: Start from the beginning.

F

Focus: Give working attention to a process, goal, or task.

G

Graphologists: Assess a person's cursive writing style and character from their handwriting.

H

Household: The number of all people living in a house or an apartment.

I

Information: Something learned from various sources.

Illiteracy: Not able to read and write.

Insurance: A policy that protects against loss of property, life, or illness.

L

Label: A fixture of a note used to identify a project, folder, or item of interest.

Learn: Understanding from experience, reading, or learning through practice to gain knowledge.

M

Medicine: Drugs with a prescription issued by a doctor for one's exclusive use.

N

Nonreader: A person that cannot read in their primary language.

Numeracy: Basic skills to read understand and work with basic numbers.

P

Penmanship: Individual writing style.

Periodic: A task that is reviewed at certain intervals throughout a plan.

Precaution: Prepare in advance to prevent unpleasant issues or events.

Program: A system of steps you do to complete a task.

Population: The number of people, money, or items counted to determine the amount.

Philanthropic: Tasks or aid given for humanitarian reasons.

R

Read: Understand the meaning of written or printed matter.

Recipe: Instruction for making various food dishes systematically.

Record: Set down in writing or copy information from mechanical means.

Retain: To receive, hold or keep.

Retirement: Age that person voluntarily stops work and has a retirement income.

S

Sauté: Foods prepared with a small amount of fat.

Session: A series of meetings to learn a skill or task.

Skill: Knowledge, training, or practice to perform a task.

Survival: Life after an event.

T

Training: Prepare or condition for an event or prepare one for life issues.

Tutor: A person that gives individual remedial instruction to individuals.

U

Unemployed: A person that does not have paid work.

V

Veteran: Experience in a task or service.

Volunteer: Perform a task or service without pay.

W

Welfare: Someone that can receive aid because of unemployment or poverty.

Write: Correctly inscribe words on paper.

REFERENCES

"He who learns teaches."
Ethiopian Proverb

Adult Literacy pic (2020) Retrieved May 15, 2019.
https://thefutureofpublishing.com/new/wp-content/uploads/2010/12/adult_literacy.jpg

Bales, K. (2019) 7 Independent Reading Activities to Increase Literacy. Retrieved January 31, 2020, from
https://www.thoughtco.com/independent-reading-activities-to-increase-literacy-4178873

Bureau of Labor Statistics (n. d.), U.S. Department of Labor, Occupational Outlook. Retrieved January 31, 2020, from *www.bls.gov/ooh.html*

Chen, J. (2018) Teaching nontraditional adult students: Adult learning theories in practice. Retrieved August 31, 2019, from *ProQuest*

Dang, T. N. Y., & Webb, S. (2016). Essential Word List. Retrieved May 27, 2021, from
https://www.edu.uwo.ca/faculty-profiles/docs/other/webb/essential-word-list.pdf

Fienberg, M. (2010) What Reading Level Is Your Bible?
https://margaretfeinberg.com/studying-the-bible-reader-levels-of-different-translations/

Find A Book (n. d.) Retrieved May 27, 2021, from
https://hub.lexile.com/find-a-book/search

Fleming, G. (2019) Calculating Reading Level With the Flesch-Kincaid Scale *https://www.thoughtco.com/calculating-reading-level-1857103*

Fire, Devon (n. d.) What Does Dysgraphia Look Like in Adults?
https://Additutemag.com/dysgraphia-in-adukts-recognizing-symptoms-later-in-life/

Garcia, A. (2013) the Many Forms of Literacy August 22, 2019, from
https://thecurrent.educatorinnovator.org/resource_section/the-many-forms-of-literacy

Gonor, A (2019) What Your Handwriting Reveals About Your Personality.
Retrieved February 21, 2020, from
https://www.womenworking.com/what-your-handwriting-reveals-about-your-personality

Hurley, A. (n. d.). AZ Quotes. Retrieved December 17, 2019, from
www.azquotes.com

Illiteracy in America (n.d.) Retrieved May 15, 2020, from
https://literacymattersworldwide.weebly.com/united-states-of-america.html

Imel, S. (1990) Alt Learner Literacy Assessment October 19, 2019, from
Eric Digest no. 103

Klein-Collins, R. (2011) Strategies for Becoming Adult-Learning-Focused
Institutions

August 16, 2019, from
http://search.proquest.com.ezproxy.trident.edu:2048/printviewfile?accountid=28844

Klemm, W. (2015). The Learning Skills Cycle: A Way to Rethink
Education Reform
https://www.psychologytoday.com/us/blog/memory-medic/201502/improve-reading-hand-eye-coordination-learning-cursive

Knowles, M. (1970). The Modern Practice of Adult Education. Retrieved
August 4, 2018, from
ProQuest

Knowles, M. (1975). Self-directed learning. New York Association Press.

Landau Susan M. Landau; Shawn M. Marks; Elizabeth C. Mormino; et al (2012). How Crossword Puzzles May Keep Alzheimer's Away.
https://www.alzinfo.org/articles/crossword-puzzles-alzheimers/

Laubach, F., Mooney, E., Laubach, R. (2011). Laubach Way to Reading. New Readers Press (p.5). New York

Loeb, Gerald (1990, April 19). Sergeant Takes on Challenge of Illiteracy. Chronicle, p. 5

Medical Dictionary, © 2009 Farley, and Partners Retrieved August 26, 2019, from
https://medicaldictionary.thefreedictionary.com/life+skills

Moser, C. (1996) Urban poverty: how do households adjust? In Ecuador Poverty Report (Washington, DC: The World Bank), p. 140.

National Assessment of Adult Literacy (2003). U.S. Department of Education, Institute of Education Sciences, National Center for Education Statistics.
https://necs.ed.gov/naal/estimates/stateEstimates.aspx

Neel, Armon (2016) Caution! These 10 Drugs Can Cause Memory Loss
https://www.aarp.org/health/drugs-supplements/info-2017/caution-these-10-drugs-can-cause-memory-loss.html

New Readers Press 1986. The Laubach Way to Reading
https://nces.ed.gov/pubs2019/2019179.pdf

Organization of Economic Cooperation and Development (2013). Adult Literacy in the United States
https://nces.ed.gov/surveys/piaac

ProLiteracy (n .d.)

http://proliteracy.org/Adult-Literacy-Facts

Readability Calculator (n. d.)
http://www.goodcalculator.com

Ritt, Martin (1990). Stanley and Iris.
https://www.imdb.com/title/tt0100680/

Sadwith, James (1987). Bluffing It.
https://interviews.televisionacademy.com/shows/bluffing-it

Self-Directed Learning. (n. d.) Segen's Medical Dictionary. (2011). Retrieved August 26, 2019 From
https://medical-dictionary.thefreedictionary.com/self-directed+learning

Social Security Administration (n. d.) Code of Federal Regulations. Retrieved January 10, 2021, from
https://www.ssa.gov/OP_Home/cfr20/404/404-1564.htm

Strong, James (n. d.) Strong's Exhaustive Concordance of the Bible

Seuss, Dr. (1940) Horton Hatches the Egg, Random House Publishers

The History of the GED (n.d.). Learning Path.Org. Retrieved May 29, 2021.
https://learningpath.org/articles/The_History_of_the_GED.html#

Tutor Training Guide (n. d.). 2011

Typing Club (n. d.) Learn Typing Free. Retrieved May 30, 2021from
https://www.typingclub.com/